How to Stop
BED
Wetting

Become the
Boss of the Bladder

Dr Janet Hall

The Five Mile Press

CONGRATULATIONS
The Boss of the Bladder Program works!
You are now dry!

Mrs Powell, Hampton, Vic.: Excellent, and beyond anything we had thought possible - we regret that we had not known about the program earlier.

Mr and Mrs Valsamis, Doncaster, Vic.: Such a serious problem solved in such a short time and with no embarrassment or discomfort to the parents or family. The best program we could have had for our son.

Mrs Lyn Kirby, Ferntree Gully,Vic.: After years of nightly bed-wetting, my twelve-year-old son was dry within twelve nights and my nine-year-old son was dry within six weeks. This was a result of combining understanding with the application of the pad and alarm system.

Mrs Cheryl Fidler, Somers,Vic.: I would recommend the program without any hesitation. My son was cured in six weeks. His confidence and self-esteem have improved in leaps and bounds. His school work has improved and he now plays competitive sport. The program was a lifesaver.

Mrs Morgan, Sale, Vic.: Our son was wetting the bed every night and sometimes several times a night. We had tried everything; medication (Tofranil), decreasing fluid intake, emptying the bladder several times before bed, waking our son during the night to take him to the toilet, cutting out sweets, raising the foot of the bed and a star chart. The results of the program were very successful. Our son's school work has improved and he is now confident and very pleased with himself.

Mrs Pierini, Balwyn, Vic.: The program has given our son a lot more confidence and he can now stay overnight at friends' houses without worrying.

ACKNOWLEDGEMENTS

Thank you to all the children and parents who contributed to the knowledge contained in this book.

Thank you to:

Neil Matterson, Jan Matthews, Peter Coote, Janet Chase, Dr Martin Knapp, Kay Farish, Pamela and Robin Hall, Robyn Glover, Michelle Moore, Pamela Tipping, Dr David Smith, Valda and Bert Ruddick, Neil Davies, and especially to Leigh Hay and Jill Branagan

ADVICE ON USING THIS BOOK

The first section of this book is to be read to young children or for older children to read to themselves. It aims to give the child the critical elements for successful management and prevention of wetting. That is – the motivation, the functional knowledge and the encouragement to take control.

The second section of this book is directed to parents, although some children may still find it interesting to read. It provides facts about learning dryness and makes specific recommendations for parents.

The third section describes the types of treatment which may be sought from professionals and gives some direction as to their effectiveness.

BOSS OF THE BLADDER

Some kids wake
To an early morning call.
Some kids have difficulty
Waking at all!
Some wake grumpy,
In a huff or a muddle,
And more than a few
Wake lying in a puddle.

Bedding wet,
Smelling PJs,
These kids would give anything
To change their ways.
Their bladder and brain
Need a hotline put through
To get the message ...
'QUICK – GO FIND A LOO!'

Imagine how pleased
These kids would be
To know in advance
When they need to do wee.
Should these kids decide
They want to be dry,
Then the rest is easy
They just have to try.

So if you know a kid
Who wets the bed,
Tell them not to despair
But be happy instead!
Tell them you read this book
And you're a whole lot gladder
'Cos now you know
How to be boss of the bladder!

The Five Mile Press Pty Ltd
1 Centre Road, Scoresby
Victoria 3179 Australia
www.fivemile.com.au

First published in 1995
Revised and updated by Pennon Publishing in 2003
This edition published by The Five Mile Press Pty Ltd in 2009
Produced for The Five Mile Press Pty Ltd by Pennon Publishing
www.pennon.com.au

Printed in Australia by Griffin Press
Cover design by Aimee Zumis
Cover photograph copyright © iStockphoto/iofoto
Page design by Allan Cornwell
Illustrations by Neil

National Library of Australia cataloguing-in-publication data

Author: Hall, Janet.

Title: How to stop bed wetting : become the boss of the bladder /
Dr Janet Hall.

ISBN: 9781742116310 (pbk.)

Subjects: Enuresis.
Urinary incontinence in children. Bladder – Physiology.
Toilet training.

Dewey Number: 649.62

CONTENTS

SECTION 1

FOR CHILDREN

HOW YOU CAN BE
BOSS OF THE BLADDER

THE BRAIN IS THE BOSS OF THE BODY

WHAT IS A BOSS?

A boss knows what to do. A policeman is the boss of traffic and a builder is the boss of making a new house.

A boss does not have to be a bossy-boots. The best kind of boss teaches other people what to do and then lets them do it by themselves. A school teacher can be a good boss for children. So can parents. But the best boss for children is their own brain.

THE BRAIN IS THE BOSS OF THE BODY

Most children's brains are good at bossing their bodies when they are learning things. They are busy learning how to play, run, skip, ride bikes, read and write. Their brains teach their bodies and then let the body parts do the work by themselves. After a body has learnt to do something, the work is done automatically. Automatic means it happens by itself.

This is the big boy or girl whose brain has to learn how to be 'Boss of the Bladder'

THE BRAIN AND THE BLADDER

Because the brain is the boss of the body it has to learn how to be the boss of the bladder. The brain is inside the head, and the bladder is inside the middle of the body. The bladder collects and holds leftover water. Some people call this water wees. (You may have a different name for it.)

HOW THE BLADDER GETS THE WEES

Food and drink go into the mouth and to the stomach. The stomach gets the goodness out and sends it through the blood to the rest of the body. The kidneys make sure the leftover water is put into the bladder. When the bladder is full, the wees is squeezed out of the body.

How the Brain, Body and Bladder Work

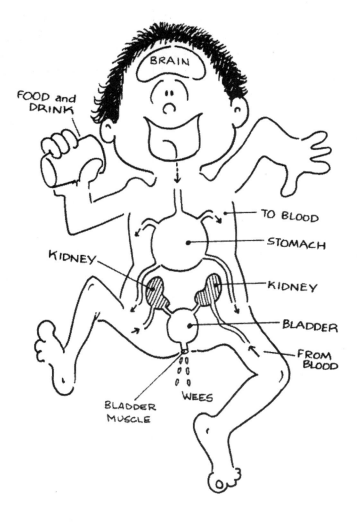

BOSS OF THE BLADDER

Some children have a problem with their bodies. THEY WET themselves. Some wet their pants during the day, some wet their bed at night, and some do both! Wetting is O.K. for babies, but not for children who are learning to play, run, skip, ride bikes, read and write.

Wetting can be very messy, smelly and uncomfortable. It can also be very embarrassing. Other people may laugh and tease if they know a child is wet.

Some parents help children HIDE their wetting problem. They don't want their child to feel uncomfortable and embarrassed. But, when parents help, THEY are the boss of a child who wets. The child's own brain does not have a chance to learn to stay dry.

 The child's brain has to learn how to be
BOSS OF THE BLADDER

THE BLADDER AND THE BLADDER MUSCLE

Children who want their own brain to be the boss of their own bladder need to learn all about how the bladder works.

The bladder is a bag made out of muscle and is just like a balloon. When it is empty, it looks like a long skinny sausage. When it is full, it looks like a large balloon that has been blown up.

Do you know what happens when you blow up a balloon too much? Yes, it bursts! Well, if our bladder burst, we would be in a lot of trouble!

Luckily the bladder has a detrusor muscle at one end and its job is to hold in the wees, or let it out when the time is right. The bladder muscle is a better idea than the string which holds the air in a balloon, because the bladder muscle can hold wees in or squeeze out as much wees as it wants, whenever it wants.

The pelvic floor muscles just under the bladder 'hold everything up'. You can make your pelvic floor muscles stronger by exercising them! Ask your parents or doctor to explain how.

The bladder muscle only lets the wees out of the bladder when it is told by the brain to let it out.

BLADDER
MUSCLE

BLADDER

AGE AND THE
BLADDER MUSCLE

As you get older, your bladder muscle gets stronger. A baby's bladder muscle is not strong.

A child's bladder muscle is learning to be strong and a grown-up usually has a very strong bladder muscle.

An older person may have a bladder muscle that is getting weaker.

WHAT MAKES THE BLADDER MUSCLE ITCHY

Sickness, cold weather and 'junk' foods and drinks can also make the bladder walls itchy and twitchy. If the bladder walls start to wobble and wriggle, it makes it harder for the bladder muscle to hold on to the wees inside.

THE WEATHER AND THE BLADDER MUSCLE

Your muscle may be uncomfortable in cold weather. The cold feeling may make the muscle itchy and twitchy and want to let go of wees more often.

SICKNESS AND THE BLADDER MUSCLE

Some muscles get sick because of infections. Germs may make your muscle itchy and twitchy. The bladder muscle may let go of wees when it is itching the germs away.

The bladder muscle may tell itself, 'I am too sick. Oh, oh! I don't care about my job of finding out if the bladder is full and then telling the brain.'

FOOD AND DRINK AND THE BLADDER MUSCLE

Some foods and drinks are very sugary and have lots of acid. Things like lollies, sweet buns, juices and lemonades may make the bladder muscle itchy and twitchy.

Caffeine in coffee or cola drinks also make the bladder muscle very itchy and could make the wees squirt out more often and at the wrong time.

THE BRAIN AND THE BLADDER MUSCLE NEED TO TALK!

When the bladder is full of wees, the nerves attached to the bladder walls and the bladder muscle send a message to the brain. The brain decides if the body is ready to let go of wees.

The stretchy bladder walls and the bladder muscle are connected to nerves which send messages to the brain. Nerves are like very fine ropes which carry 'talking' signals to and fro from the brain and the body.

The brain and the bladder muscle need to talk. When the bladder is full, the bladder walls give a squeeze, and tell the bladder muscle. Then the nerves carry the message to the brain that the child wants to wee. The child's brain can be in control if it can talk to the bladder muscle and make it hold on to the wees.

The brain tells the bladder muscle when to let go

THE BRAIN/BLADDER MUSCLE TALK MAY NOT WORK – THE MUSCLE MAY BE SICK OR TIRED

Sometimes the muscle does not get the message from the full bladder. The muscle may be sick or tired. It may just let go.

YOUR BRAIN MAY NOT BE LISTENING TO THE BLADDER MUSCLE TALK

Sometimes a strong and healthy bladder muscle cannot get the brain to listen to it. The muscle may be too busy doing something else like reading or playing. For children who wet their bed at night, the brain may be asleep.

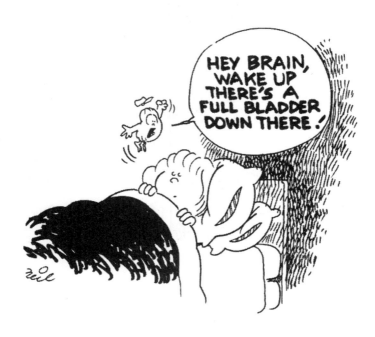

THE SIZE OF
THE BLADDER

Bladders come in different sizes. Let's call them sizes 1 to 10. Some people are born with small bladders. No matter how much they stretch they will only ever be size 5. Some people are born with big bladders which are stretchy. They can stretch to size 10.

THE BLADDER NEEDS TO BE STRETCHED AS MUCH AS IT CAN

Some bladders could be bigger but have never been stretched.

You can measure how stretchy your bladder is by drinking lots, holding on as long as you can, then weeing into a measuring jug. The jug will show how many milli-litres (ml) you can hold in your bladder. A child's stretchy bladder might usually hold about 250 ml. Usually an adult can hold from 300 to 400 ml.

If you pour 250 ml of water into a measuring jug you will be able to see just how much wees a stretchy bladder might be able to hold.

WETTING CAN BE CATCHY

Children whose parents or family wet the bed when they were young may be more likely to wet the bed too! Just as some children get their hair and eye colour from their parents, they can also get their parents' small bladder and weak bladder muscle.

This is how bedwetting can be catchy - you might catch it from your parents!

WORRY AND THE BLADDER

Getting a fright or being very worried can often make the bladder muscle twitch and the wees will come out by accident.

Some people would need a very big fright, like getting chased by a savage dog, before their muscle would get scared enough to let go. Other people get scared of more everyday things like grumpy teachers, spelling tests or school concerts, and that makes their muscle twitch. After a while, simply thinking about scary things can make some people worry – their bladder muscle twitches and they wet.

Sometimes a bad fright can make someone wet

Even children who stay dry during the day can sometimes get worried at night. Their brains are busy dreaming about scary or worrying things. When the bladder muscle can't get the brain to listen, it lets go and the child wets the bed. This probably happens more with some older children who wet the bed. Their brains are very good at worrying but not so good at telling the bladder muscle who is the boss during the night.

Some DRY people think that people who wet must be lazy. This is silly! Hardly anyone would ever want to wet on purpose! (Perhaps just one or two children have wet on purpose just to make their parents feel bad or uncomfortable!)

Maybe a child might be angry with his parents for separating and getting a divorce. This is very rare. It is more likely that the child's worry about his parents being unhappy, makes him wet.

Some children worry that by wetting, they upset their parents

WETTING
IS COMMON

Many children take a while to learn to be dry. No-one seems to mind if a child wets during the day or night when he or she is little. But by the time of going to kindergarten, everyone expects a child to be able to stay dry all day and most nights.

By the time a child goes to school, people expect dry pants in the day and a dry bed all night. Most school children are dry during the day but one in ten, up to the age of ten, still wets the bed at night. That means that in every grade, at least two children may wet the bed. It is not strange that no-one knows who the two children are. They keep it a secret so that they will not be teased.

Would you want everyone in your grade to know that you wet the bed?

BEING WET IS UNCOMFORTABLE

The results of being wet are very uncomfortable. Wetting feels cold, is sticky and often smelly. If you wet in the daytime you have to change your clothes and maybe clean the floor and have a wash. If you wet at night you have to change both your pyjamas and the bed and then have a wash. This is no fun in the middle of the night, especially in winter!

If other children find out that you wet, they may tease you. So you may not want to go to school camp or sleep over at a friend's house if you wet. You might be very embarrassed.

Some children who have wet for a long time think they are not a good person. A feeling of not being a good person is called low self-esteem. Children with low self-esteem do not like themselves because they do not know how to make the brain be the boss of the bladder. They can get very embarrassed about many other everyday things and act very shy.

Parents get very worried if their child has low self-esteem. They may nag the child to be dry because they know this will make him feel better. Parents don't realise that this only adds pressure and makes the child feel worse.

Some parents do mean and nasty things like making the child have a cold shower, calling the child names like 'smelly' or 'stinky', or even rubbing their noses in the wet like a puppy dog – but only a few parents do that! Most parents are very kind and understanding.

TWO WAYS
TO STAY DRY

There may be two kinds of people who stay dry all night. One is a 'get-up' person, and one is a 'shut-up' person.

A 'GET-UP' PERSON

People with small bladders have to get up during the night. Perhaps their bladder cannot hold onto wees for the time that they are sleeping. Their brains have to learn to listen to the bladder muscle and wake up the person and take them to the toilet.

A 'SHUT-UP' PERSON

'Shut-up' people are the lucky ones. Their bladder can learn to stretch when their bladder muscle tells the brain that they're getting full up. The brain can tell the bladder muscle to shut-up and hold on to the wees all night. That lucky person can wake up feeling really comfortable and refreshed next morning.

Which do you think you would be: A 'Get-up' or a 'Shut-up' Person?

It doesn't really matter which, so long as you have a dry and comfortable night.

HOW CAN PARENTS HELP?

The first step in becoming dry is WANTING to become dry.

Children usually need help from a grown-up to stay dry. The main thing, however, is that you want to get dry just for yourself.

Your parents can give you heaps of encouragement. Ask them about a star chart or a calender tick program. You could also make sure that you practise all the things that you need to do to take care of yourself when you go to the toilet, and all the things that you need to do to tidy up if you do have a wetting accident.

Your parents might help you by asking a special doctor or other consultant (that's a special person who knows how to help) to let you have the use of a machine which has an alarm that rings whenever your bed is wet.

DO NOT TAKE THE CHILD TO THE TOILET DURING THE NIGHT

Some parents think they are helping the child stay dry by lifting the child out of bed at some time during the night. They put the child on the toilet and because there is sometimes a wees, the parents think they have helped.

Actually they do not help for two reasons.

1. The first reason the parents should not take the child to the toilet is that the child is not really awake when he is put on the toilet!

   The parent's brain is bossing the child's sleepy brain.

   The child's brain is not being the boss.

The child's bladder muscle has not talked to the brain.

   The child's brain has not noticed the need to go to the toilet.

If the child's brain is not being the BOSS OF THE BLADDER, the child will not learn to STAY DRY.

In fact ... the child might learn:
'When I'm half asleep I should wet!'

2. The second reason the parents should not take the child to the toilet is that the bladder bag is not having a chance to stretch. Every time the parent lifts and takes the child to the toilet, the bladder is emptying and will keep being a small-sized bladder.

Maybe it will never be stretched enough!

DO NOT STOP THE CHILD FROM DRINKING

Another thing parents think they are doing to help children who wet at night is to stop drinks in the late afternoon or before bed. This only makes the child uncomfortably thirsty and may cause the parent and child to argue. The child thinks it is not fair!

Remember, stopping drinks may stop the bladder size from learning to stretch and get bigger.

Also, if drinking slows down, the wees may become more smelly and can make the bladder walls and muscle itchy.

This can cause more wetting.

EXTRA DRINKS

Extra drinks are a great idea for children who wet. Extra drinks help their bladder stretch to the maximum size!

You could still expect wet beds at first, of course, but after a while the stretchy bladder could hold any sized drinks and still make sure the child could stay dry.

Extra drinks train the bladder to hold on

FORGETTING HOW
TO STAY DRY

Some children find that they get dry but it doesn't last long. They are very disappointed when they start to wet again. They have to learn dryness again. This is just like a test. The test is to make sure that when you get dry the second time, you really feel good about your win over the annoying wetting problem.

If you get dry but then wet again, it may be that your brain and body are very busy learning other new things. They just forget to co-operate!

Just take a deep breath and decide to go back to whatever you did in the first place to get dry and pretty soon you will be feeling happy and comfortable again.

A CHECKLIST
FOR CHILDREN

Now we know about the bladder, we can think about why some children might wet. Tick off the box if you think the reason might fit you.

☐ Bladder size: You were born with a small bladder. Even when it is stretched to the limit, it is only a size 5. If you don't know your bladder size, measure it! How many ml does it hold?

☐ Your bladder is not stretched enough. You can't hold on during school, or out shopping, or all night in bed.

☐ Your bladder muscle is weak.

☐ Your bladder muscle is sick. Your parents may need to take you to the doctor to find out if you have an infection.

☐ Your bladder muscle does not send the message to your brain.

☐ Your brain does not listen to your bladder muscle's message. If you wet the bed, this may be because you are a deep sleeper.

☐ You worry a lot.

☐ You have a low self-esteem.
(That is, you don't like yourself much.)

SECTION **2**

FOR PARENTS

HOW YOU CAN BE
BOSS OF THE BLADDER

INTRODUCTION

It is a source of amazement to me that we have man on the moon and yet do not know how to predictably prevent a child from day- and night-wetting.

In twenty-five years of treating hundreds of children, adolescents and adults, I have been increasingly amazed by the amount of variation which is shown in types of wetting and types of treatment and its effectiveness.

It is my belief that **the key factors** in gaining long-term dryness are **child self-esteem, knowledge and motivation**.

Children need to **want** to be dry to feel good about their own sense of personal power.

The critical elements for successful management and prevention of wetting are:

1. The child is motivated to be dry.
2. The child has functional knowledge of the basic bodily processes involved in wetting and in staying dry.
3. The child is encouraged to take control; adults are only assisting.

THE CHILD IS THE GAME PLAYER AND HAS THE BALL. THE PARENT BARRACKS FROM THE SIDELINE. THE PROFESSIONAL IS THE COACH.

DO NOT LABEL
THE CHILD

The practice of putting labels on children tends to promote a self-fulfilling prophecy. For instance, a red-haired child called 'stroppy' may well develop a fiery temper. Calling the child 'a bedwetter' can doom him to a belief that his behaviour is out of his control. The bedwetter label damns the doer, rather than the deed. Children need to know they do have control; they also need to know they have unconditional love. You wouldn't call a child who was learning to ride a bike a 'bike-faller'. You would call him a bike-riding learner. It is recommended that a child experiencing problems with wetting is called a 'dryness learner'.

FACTS ABOUT
BLADDER CONTROL

TERMS
Involuntary wetting is called 'enuresis'. Day-wetting is called 'diurnal enuresis' and night-wetting is called 'nocturnal enuresis'.

DAY CONTROL
Awareness of the results of wetting (wet pants or puddles) usually begins at about 15 months. Awareness of internal sensations of the need to pass urine can occur from 20 months. Most children, by the age of three-and-a-half, have learned to recognise the sensation of a full bladder and hold on until at a potty or toilet. By the age of five, children can voluntarily pass urine even if their bladder is not full.

DAY CONTROL AND TRAINING

Day control can be developed with training, but this needs to be appropriate to the child's developmental stage. Methods of toilet training are many and varied, with a background of amazing folklore. My book *Easy Toilet Training* gives a solid understanding of the most positive approach to toilet training.

NIGHT CONTROL

By the age of four years, seventy per cent of children are dry at night most of the time. By age five, fifteen per cent of children still wet the bed. By age ten, seven per cent of children still wet the bed, and by age fifteen, only one per cent wet at night.

NIGHT CONTROL AND TRAINING

Night control usually develops later than day control and does not necessarily respond to special training. Night control develops gradually over months. Since night control develops naturally, it is important that parents avoid pressure on day training. Methods which are stressful, over-controlling or involve punishment, are not recommended.

TYPES OF NIGHT-WETTING

It is likely that there are three different types of night-wetting

PRIMARY NIGHT-WETTING:
Primary enuresis describes children who have never had a dry night.

INTERMITTENT NIGHT-WETTING:
The child has had occasional dry nights, but wets most of the time.

SECONDARY NIGHT-WETTING:
Some children may be reliably dry for a considerable time (months to years) and then start to wet again. This is called secondary enuresis.

BLADDER CAPACITY

By the age of two years, a child is usually able to hold urine for a brief period.

By the age of four-and-a-half years, the bladder capacity in most children has doubled, and should be sufficient to hold the nightly output of urine.

FUNCTIONAL BLADDER CAPACITY
Some children with enuresis do have a small bladder capacity, but some children with good bladder control may have a small functional capacity. Taking an interest in measurements of bladder capacity and if small, attempting to increase it, are helpful in achieving a better awareness of the bladder and urination control.

THROW OUT THE FAIRYTALES ABOUT WETTING

 FAIRYTALE NO. 1

– There is a problem with the plumbing system

Medical investigation of physical reasons for wetting is usually limited to analysis of urine. Operations or X-rays are not usually done unless there is a very severe problem. Physical abnormalities are rare.

In two per cent of children, frequent, recurrent infections may contribute to wetting. Occasionally there is some reflux or reverse flow from the bladder to the kidneys.

To rule out possible physical problems, it is **strongly recommended** that any child with consistent wetting, inappropriate to his developmental age, is **examined medically** before any treatment is commenced.

 FAIRYTALE NO. 2

– Just wait, the child 'will grow out of it'

As developmental facts show, some children do not obtain night dryness until mid-teenage years. **They do not grow out of it easily.**

Waiting time can allow poor self-esteem to become firmly entrenched, producing long-term emotional problems and self-limiting behaviours. I believe that the longer it is left untreated, continuous bedwetting above the age of six years may contribute to psychological problems.

Why wait if relatively unobtrusive treatment methods can promote dryness in children at an early age?

I recommend that children over the age of five years are entitled to be offered a technique (which is based on substantial evidence for its effectiveness) for treatment of wetting. Such techniques are described later in this book.

 FAIRYTALE NO. 3

– Night-wetters are very deep sleepers

Research has not found that bedwetting is connected with deep sleeping. Although some bedwetting children are deep sleepers, many children who **DO NOT** wet are **ALSO** deep sleepers. Many deep sleepers manage to wake up and go to the toilet. Their brains still get the message from the bladder.

 FAIRYTALE NO. 4

– Wetting and intelligence – only slow children wet the bed

Children who wet can be fast, average or slow at learning. Some slow learners may also be slow at learning dryness, but so can many bright children.

 FAIRYTALE NO. 5

– Children who wet are just lazy and naughty

CHILDREN DO NOT WET ON PURPOSE

Children are embarrassed about their wetting and do not find it comfortable. Wetting often stings, is cold and smelly and a child can be teased because of it.

Some children, especially those with secondary enuresis, put on a show of not caring that they wet. This is only to cover up their true dislike of their problem. It is because they do not know how to gain control of dryness. Their self-esteem suffers and **they pretend** their wetting is not a problem in order to protect further breakdowns in self-esteem.

Children who remain lying in wet beds are sometimes comfortable, so long as they do not move the sheets. They try to ignore the wet in the hope it will go away.

For some young children who wet during the day, the accident is due to distraction by play. They are so busy in their play activity, they may simply not register the signal from the bladder to the brain. Some may get the message too late to actually delay wetting until they get to the toilet. Their bladder size or muscle strength may not be strong enough to delay.

With intermittent or secondary enuresis, the child's feelings of being out of control may be even more frustrating. With intermittent wetting, it is impossible for a child to predict a wetting incident. In some cases then, a child may stay awake and be **'on guard'** all night when he goes on school camp or stays with a friend, in order to prevent the embarrassment of a wet bed.

It is not surprising that children with secondary enuresis may give up on themselves in disgust when, after a long period of dryness, they suddenly start to wet. They may ask, *'What have I done to deserve this?'*

 FAIRYTALE NO. 6

– Wetting and other problems

Children who wet may also bite their nails, suffer from breathing problems like asthma, cry at sad movies and be scared of the dark.

Please note: Children WHO DO NOT WET can also have the same problems.

Some children who have traumatic experiences, like being in a car crash, house fire or hospitalised, may start to wet. Other children who have the same trauma will not develop wetting problems.

WE CANNOT PREDICT WHO WILL HAVE WETTING PROBLEMS.

 FAIRYTALE NO. 7

– A child's wetting is the parents' fault

You have not failed your child. Parents are **not** responsible for the cause of the child's wetting. If your child inherits your small bladder or 'slow to mature' nervous system, he or she may be a slow dryness learner. You cannot blame yourself for the process of heredity. Remember, your child may just as easily inherit your fine athletic or creative ability.

Parents who have restricted drinks and lifted the child, have done so with the very best intentions. However, now that you know that these procedures are not helpful in the long term, please discontinue them.

WHAT PARENTS
CAN DO

Often a caring parent will attempt to shield the child from the negative consequences of wetting. For instance, the parent would cuddle the wet child, change the child's bed and then allow the child to share the parent's bed.

This approach may, in fact, serve as a reward for continued wetting.

Parental comfort and attention, and even sharing the bed, could well outweigh the negative effects of wetting. More importantly, this approach takes away from the child's sense of self-control. The child sees the parent as being the director of all management and does not feel that there is any personal power in preventing or handling the consequences of wetting.

BE MATTER OF FACT

Parents need to have a matter-of-fact approach to handling wetting and the encouraging expectancy of dryness. Children need to be encouraged to manage the consequences of wetting by themselves. It is important that the management of wetting is seen as a natural consequence and not as a punishment.

MANAGEMENT OF WETTING

It is also important that management tasks suit the child's developmental stage. For instance, it is reasonable that a three-year-old child could mop up the wet spot and take his or her wet knickers to the laundry.

It is reasonable to expect that an eight-year-old could take the wet bed clothes to the laundry, independently take a shower or bath, and assist the parent in making the bed with fresh sheets.

It is reasonable that a ten-year-old be totally responsible for managing wet beds.

Parents need to decide what is reasonable for their child.

REWARDS CAN BE USED WITH CAUTION

Star charts or calendar programs involve daily records of dry or wet incidents, where sometimes rewards are exchangeable for a certain number of dry days or nights. Pep talks, star charts and calendars have a success rate of about twenty-five per cent.

Traditionally, well-meaning parents have offered rewards to their children for dryness. This works well in many cases for children who are almost dry. However, rewards are inappropriate for children who have never learned to be dry. In this case, the rewards can cause more stress.

DO NOT PUNISH

Never criticise, punish or embarrass your child for wetting. Parents who use punishment in toilet training or handling wet beds may, in fact, be contributing to continued wetting. The child who is fearful of parental reaction may worry about this, and this worry may contribute to continued wetting.

RECORDS

Keeping any sort of consistent record is a useful thing for parents to do. Records can clearly show the child's progress over time. Records can also serve as a guide in devising a suitable treatment program. In addition to recording occasions of wetting, it may be useful to record occasions of bowel use. Constipation has been associated with wetting, where compacted bowel matter presses on the bladder. The doctor would be interested in any records which show a history of constipation. The parent could help in preventing constipation by encouraging the child to eat a nutritious diet and drink normal amounts of fluid.

Keep records – you never know how useful they can be.

DO NOT RESTRICT LIQUIDS

In Section 1, it was explained that lifting the child (wake and take) and restricting fluids really serve only to limit development of maximal bladder capacity.

Increase, don't decrease liquids.

Increased liquid intake is to be encouraged, no matter what method of treatment is used. At first, wetting may be more likely but as the bladder enlarges, the increased capacity will promote less frequent wetting incidents.

DIET

There is some controversy as to whether foods high in preservatives and food colourings may cause wetting. Each parent needs to assess the possible relationship between types of foods and wetting in the light of the individual circumstances of child and parent. That is, manage your child's food and drink intake according to the results that you observe. A child may often be more likely to wet at night after a party, but it would not be clear as to whether this was due to excess intake of sweet foods or to the excitement of the special occasion.

INFLUENCES ON
WETTING

The following have been noted to contribute sometimes to the slow learning of dryness in children:

 inappropriate toilet lighting

 long distance to the toilet

 clothing difficult to manage

 cold air

 unable to read the signs

 no light source in the dark

 noisy plumbing pipes

CONSTIPATION

In a few children, constipation can be an influence on bedwetting. Perhaps the compacted faeces put pressure on the bladder? Constipation should first be treated with a good diet and increased fluids. If it becomes chronic, it can cause 'overflow' leakage which soils pants and bedding and can bring emotional upset for the child and parents. A very useful book for addressing this problem is *Beating Sneaky Poo* by Terry Heins and Karen Ritchie. Please see the reference section in the back of this book if you wish to get your own copy.

SELF-MANAGED TOILET VISITS MAY BE A PREREQUISITE FOR STAYING DRY AT NIGHT

There are some basic skills needed for a child to be able to visit the toilet during the night. Parents should **not assume** the child has these skills. It could be useful to test him by turning out lights in the house when the child is in bed and asking him to show you how to get to the toilet. This could involve:

1. Getting to the toilet.
    This could be a game. Count how many steps you take. Can you walk them like a robot would? Can you walk them like a ghost would? Sing a song and skip.

2. Turning the toilet light on and off.

3. Getting back into bed.

4. To reassure a child who was timid in the dark, you could scatter a trail of soft toys from the bed to the toilet. The child could follow the familiarly reassuring soft toy trail safely to and from the toilet.

WETTING AND WORRY

Often, wetting is the horse and worry or upset is the cart. That is, primary enuresis occurs first, and a child worries about the wetting. It is understandable that a child who has never experienced a dry night may worry about being different. Feeling out of control, the child will be frustrated that friends have no wetting problems and they don't need to put effort into staying dry.

The more upset a child becomes, the more chance he has of wetting. It just becomes a vicious cycle and the wetting may be even more difficult to cure.

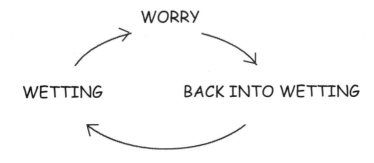

WORRY

WETTING

BACK INTO WETTING

TOILET TRAINING FOR DAYTIME

TOILET TRAINING TODDLERS

Please read my book *Easy Toilet Training* (companion edition to this book) for a full description of toilet training.

A book called *Toilet Training in Less Than a Day* by Azrin and Foxx may inspire confident parents to attempt to train their toddler in a day. In my experience, training can take a few days, weeks and sometimes much longer!

The procedure that is recommended requires intensive practise of skills that are needed for toileting. The most important thing to remember is that the practise, indeed all of the training, should be done in a sense of fun, curiosity and discovery.

There is a likelihood that very early toilet training (before eighteen months) is not helpful and could even delay control.

CHILDREN WHO HAVE BEEN DRY, AND BEGIN TO HAVE WET KNICKERS

Some children who have been trained very early and been successfully dry for some time (perhaps years) begin to come home from kindergarten, or even school, with wet knickers.

At first the child may be embarrassed and pretend that the knickers were not very wet at all. As the incidents increase, the wetting becomes an obvious concern to the child, parent and teacher. Eventually the child may be totally unaware of the wetting problem. Fortunately other children are often very kind and ignore wetting. Occasionally they can be very hurtful by teasing the wet child.

Some of the possible reasons for returning to day wetting are as follows:

1. The child never learned proper toileting skills in the first place.
2. The child receives a lot of attention for being wet. Negative attention may be rewarding – the child may be seeking some kind of power over his caregivers by saying, *'I'll make you care about me, look what a fuss I've caused.'*
3. There may be a new baby in the family, or at least some sibling competition. The child who wets may feel left out.
4. Diet change; for instance increased citrus juice, may contribute towards wetting.
5. The child may have a negative reaction to the toilet. Sometimes the toilet may be very cold and dark, with spider webs and holes in the walls (this may be particularly true of school toilets). The child may have developed some negative attitude to what he perceives as a nasty place and a nasty, dirty or at least inconvenient behaviour, to have to perform. This child may have a particularly tidy personality.

6. Occasionally children refuse to go to the toilet during the day at school because other children tease them. Some children hold on all day at school and are 'busting' by home time.
7. The child is so enthusiastic about playing that he postpones going to the toilet for so long that his bladder muscle refuses to co-operate and lets go of the wees. Bad bladder habits may lead to bladder irritability and ongoing wetting.

BASIC PROCEDURES FOR DAYTIME TRAINING

Basic procedures for daytime training are that the child learns by:

 Imitation

 Practise

 Mild consequences

 A motivation program of stickers, stars and rewards

 A prompting procedure

These above procedures will be explained in detail below.
First of all the parents must be aware of the prerequisites which are required to indicate readiness for dryness.

PREREQUISITES

1. Does the child let go of a convincing amount of urine at one go? You might like to test the bladder capacity by measuring total ml. Toddlers may have a capacity of less

than 100 ml and yet still be ready to learn to self-toilet and stay dry during the day.

2. Are there periods of dryness for the child between nappy changes?

3. Does the child know the meaning of the words *'wet'* and *'dry'*?

4. Can the child follow at least five different instructions?

5. Can the child:

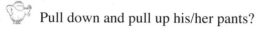 Pull down and pull up his/her pants?

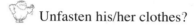 Unfasten his/her clothes?

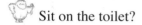 Sit on the toilet?

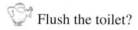 Flush the toilet?

 Wash and dry hands?

Prior to attempting training, the following procedures are recommended:

1. MATERIALS

The child gets used to having a pot in the room.
The parent collects materials that will be used:

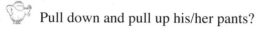 A doll

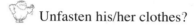 Clean changes of knickers

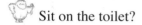 Supplies of different kinds of drinks the child likes

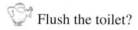 Supplies of different snacks the child likes

A list of people who will be excited to learn that the child is being dry. Azrin and Foxx call this, 'The Friends Who Care List'.

2. Foods

It is recommended that the child not be given breakfast that morning, but be given lots of drinks and even salty foods, so that she will want to drink more. Foods that are readily available in Australia include: Twisties, Cheezels, sultanas, Rice Bubbles, Coco Pops, jellybeans and Smarties.

Please note that this is not a recommendation to fill your child up for any long period with junk foods. All of these foods can be cut up into very small pieces. One jellybean can be cut up into eight pieces. All that is needed is enough of the food to be placed on the child's tongue, so that the child gets that instant *'hit'* of good taste.

As soon as the program practises have finished there is **no** need to give further foods, and it would certainly **not be** recommended beyond two days.

TOILET TRAINING PROCEDURES

Specific procedures for these fun days of toilet training are as follows:

LEARN BY IMITATION

(a) **Co-operation: Successful wee on pot by toy.**
Choose a toy that the child may particularly like to be the demonstrator of successful toileting. The child is to learn by imitation. You may get a dolly who wets from the toy shop. These dolls have a hole in the crutch and you can actually pour liquid in the mouth and it will come out of the hole. However, any toy will do.

Dolly is to sit on the toilet, have a drink and wee into the pot. Dolly is to wet on the pot successfully on three occasions. The parent acts out **how pleased he or she is,** and gives the dolly a snack. Of course, dolly can't eat the snack, and so the child gets the snack as a reward!

(b) **The parent models successful toileting.**
Parent successfully practises wetting on pot or toilet in front of the child three times. Choose a time early in the day when you'll have no interruptions.

(c) **The child practises successful toileting.**
The child is to practise talking out aloud using the pot. The child can be the parent practising with the doll, or doing it him/herself. The parent may have a small glass of liquid which can be poured into the pot which can be the pretend wees, depending on whether the child enjoys that pretence.

WHAT TO DO WITH ACCIDENTS

(a) **Dolly has an accident.**
With the doll, the parent practises three times the procedure for handling accidents. When the doll's knickers are checked, the parent says *'Oh, dolly's wet.'*

In a firm disapproving tone the parent says, *'No dolly, I don't like wet pants.'*

Azrin and Foxx recommend a procedure called 'positive practice' where the doll is then required to practise three times moving quickly to the toilet, pulling down knickers, sitting down, standing up, pulling knickers back up, washing hands and going back to play.

In my experience this can be a particularly negative situation, with conflict and tears between parent and child. It would be recommended, however, that the doll demonstrates responsibility for the wet pants. This requires changing the wet knickers, putting the wet knickers in the laundry and perhaps washing them, and cleaning up whatever wet may have been on the floor.

At all times, it is stressed that the parent needs to be matter of fact, with a disapproving, but not critical or nasty tone.

(b) The child acts as the parent with the dolly and moves through three practises of what to do with dolly when wet.

PROMPTING

After the practises with the doll, the parent is ready to start prompting the child to go to the potty independently.

1. At first the prompt is very direct, for example, *'Suzie, would you sit on the potty and do wees, please?'* (half hourly).

2. After success with half-hour prompts, the next is a general question after an hour, *'Suzie, do you want to go to the potty?'*

3. Next would be a reminder at mid-morning: *'Don't forget to go to the potty, Suzie'*.

4. Finally the child would be able to self-initiate and go to the toilet whenever required.

Depending on the age of the child, previous experience with toileting and motivation, it is up to the parent to decide what type of instruction needs to be given.

MOTIVATION BY REWARDS

1.   IMMEDIATE REWARDS

Immediate rewards can be the portion of jelly bean for correct toiletings during the week. Older children may be rewarded by having five cents in a jar for each successful toileting.

Children of any age could greatly benefit from immediate praise from the parents and also from the 'Friends Who Care List'. The child could be encouraged to telephone grandparents for instance, to tell them how wonderful it was that he/she successfully used the potty. Of course, the parent should make sure that the grandparent is going to be home, and that the grandparent knows how to give lots of praise and encouragement to the child.

2.   DAILY REWARDS

For children who are successfully urinating on the toilet, but still having occasional wets during the day, a daily reward may be sufficient. This could be a star chart or some kind of sticker, which could be given nightly, if an entire dry day had been obtained.

3.   WEEKLY REWARDS

Weekly rewards, such as an outing at the end of the week, may be rewarding. In my experience, once a child has been dry for longer than a week, no more attention need be given in terms of rewards.

A CHECKLIST
FOR PARENTS

☐ Have the child medically examined by a doctor.

☐ Help your child measure the bladder capacity.

☐ Encourage your child to drink fluids as wanted.

☐ Other than a prompt before bed and after meals, let the child decide when he wants to visit the toilet.

☐ Know the facts (for example, the developmental stages of dryness) about bladder control.

☐ Encourage your child to clean up clothing, floor or bed after a wet. Say nothing directly about the wet.

☐ Praise the child for being dry.

☐ Encourage your child to eat a balanced, nutritious diet.

☐ Try to boost the child's self-esteem at all times.

☐ Encourage the child to feel in control.

ADVICE FROM THE EXPERT ON TREATMENT FOR PROBLEMS WITH WETTING

BEDWETTING MANAGEMENT AND TREATMENT

The following recommendations are made as a result of my experience at the Boss of the Bladder Program in Melbourne, Victoria.

MEDICAL ADVICE

Parents usually do not take a child to the doctor specifically for bedwetting treatment. It is more likely that a concerned parent may take the child to the doctor for some physical complaint like a viral infection, and mention the bedwetting as a persistent annoyance.

Unfortunately many doctors recommend the parents 'to just wait, the child will grow out of it'. Such advice is usually given in the best of intentions to protect the child from being pressured by anxious parents. In the long run, however, waiting may often cause extreme frustration for the child and the parent. It is especially damaging to the child's self-esteem.

As children become of primary school age, and are encouraged to go on school camps and stay overnight, bedwetting can be a particular source of embarrassment, confusion and low self-confidence.

I recommend that children from five years of age are able to be motivated and parents guided by a professional. Sometimes younger children can be treated, but usually five years of age is the minimal age for professional intervention. There are exceptions with very bright young children and extremely motivated parents, when the indicators are positive for the child learning to become dry. For instance, a child may be waking during the night distressed at the wet bed that has been causing discomfort and the reason for wakening.

DRUGS

Doctors may prescribe medication for children. The most commonly used is Tofranil. This drug acts to relax the bladder muscle so that the bladder is less likely to empty spontaneously.

Unfortunately, Tofranil is also widely prescribed as an anti-depressant for adults. Parents have reported that there are possible side effects such as hyperactivity symptoms, irritability and lethargy.

Tofranil may successfully stop a child wetting, but often the child will start wetting again as soon as the drug is withdrawn. The success rate for permanent stopping of wetting is less than forty per cent.

One child seen by me had been taking Tofranil for over three years and yet was still occasionally wetting the bed. At age eleven, an enuresis alarm and motivation program was devised and, after four weeks, the child was dry. Three months later, the mother reported that the child's grades at school had improved from a C to a B, his self-confidence had improved and he was generally more co-operative and calm.

Some doctors are now prescribing a nasal spray called Desmopressin (DDAVP) to help children stop wetting. Some children have become dry, some have become wet again when the drug is stopped and some don't get dry at all. Of greatest concern is the risk of accidental poisoning. Desmopressin is only effective when being taken, so it may be useful in helping with a social dilemma like going on a school camp. It is not a cure.

Whether you choose a drug method for treatment for your child's bedwetting depends on you and your doctor. As a mother, I would not like my child to take drugs, especially if there may be side effects and no guarantee of getting dry.

THE IMPORTANCE OF THE PROFESSIONAL COACH

The most important aspect of seeking professional supervision for bedwetting, is that of motivation. A solution to any problem can be blocked by emotional closeness between family members. A child is much more likely to become enthusiastic about a program offered by a bright and positive therapist. The child can be inspired to believe that he or she is responsible and can independently contribute to gaining dryness.

> **REMEMBER THE CHILD IS THE PLAYER,**
> **THE PROFESSIONAL IS THE COACH**
> **AND THE PARENTS ARE THE SUPPORTERS**
> **WHO STAND ON THE SIDELINES**

ENURESIS ALARMS

As a result of experience I make a strong recommendation that alarms should be used with professional supervision. The success rate under these circumstances can be as high as ninety per cent.

The alarm program which I use is suitable for a child of at least five years of age. Older children are given as much encouragement as possible to be independently responsible for managing the alarm. Weekly reports of progress are extremely important in order to maintain the child's and parents' motivation, and monitor the reliable use of the instrument. Reports can easily be managed by telephone.

There are a range of alarms available through chemists. I have repeatedly found that parents come to me for assistance after having bought a cheap alarm from the chemist and found that either the child did not awaken to the alarm, or the alarm would sound inconsistently. Parents have been woken during the night to alarm sounds which had been simply triggered by the child's perspiration. Disappointed parents and children have woken in the morning to a flooded bed when the alarm did not sound.

The Boss of the Bladder Program, established in Melbourne, uses the most efficient and reliable alarms available on the market today. These alarms are only available from professionals; usually nurses, social workers, psychologists, doctors and special teachers. The important aspects of conditioning with an alarm are that the child awakens as fully as possible, and makes a trip to the toilet (whether there has been minimal or full wetting).

The most commonly used alarm is the bell and pad. The urine sensitive rubber pad is put on the mattress and connected to a buzzer/bell alarm box near the bed. When a wet occurs, the alarm sound wakes the child, who is encouraged to finish the urinating on the toilet.

Problems with the bell and pad are rare. The exception is where the child is a very deep sleeper. With persistent parental encouragement and practise, however, the child can usually be taught to arouse to the bell. Personally worn alarms are typically used for toilet training during the day and can be used for night training. The device has a small alarm which is pinned to night clothes and connected to a small sensor that is worn in the pants. These alarms have advantages in ease of transport and cost, but reliability may need to be tested.

Parents have reported to me that 'There is nothing more frustrating than an alarm that goes off when it shouldn't and doesn't go off when it should.'

In most cases, alarms are successful within six to eight weeks. There is extreme variation for individuals, however, with permanent dry nights being gained after two nights in one instance in my practice, but not after sixteen weeks in another.

Extra drinks may be included in an alarm program. Research evidence and practical experience have indicated that children who have a series of dry nights can then be encouraged to drink more (thereby overloading the system). If they can **still** persist with dryness, they may be more likely to remain dry indefinitely.

With the introduction of extra drinks, wetting may resume for a short period, until the bladder learns to hold that amount of urine or the bladder muscle wakes the brain. In my practice, recommend extra drinks in most instances. A few exceptions are with young children who can't understand the concept of extra practice and with extremely anxious children who, once dry, are horrified at the thought of wetting again.

DAY-RETENTION
TRAINING

Children with day-wetting problems can be encouraged to play 'holding on' games.

An intense program involves increasingly longer intervals of holding on between the passing of urine. The child is asked to tell the parent when he wants to go to the toilet. The parent encourages the child to hold on. The time is gradually increased – four minutes, ten minutes, fifteen minutes, up to forty-five minutes. A kitchen timer may be used to assist the game. Ask the child 'Can you beat the buzzer?' A piece of a jellybean (one jellybean can be cut in four or even eight) can be a reward for successfully prolonging the length of the delay.

HOLDING ON GAMES AIM AT INCREASING BLADDER CAPACITY

Retention training may work in forty per cent of cases, but even when this procedure does not cure wetting, it should make other approaches easier to carry out due to increased bladder capacity. Some children can cheat by telling you they want to go before they really have the urge. They do this to make sure they will get the reward. Ongoing measurement of capacity, by having the child actually wee into a bucket or a jug, may provide a check on this attempt at manipulation. The reward would only be given if capacity showed an increase, therefore proving that the child had been holding on for some time.

Caution: Children with recurrent infections should NOT be asked to 'hold on'.

PROGRESSIVE
WAKENING

Progressive awakening is not the same as lifting the child. In lifting, or 'waking and taking', the parent wakes the child once a night, typically prior to the parent retiring to bed. Section 1 of this book discussed how waking and taking is really doing nothing in teaching the child to take control, and indeed may simply perpetuate low bladder capacity by having the child keep his bladder empty.

A regular waking program is much more systematic, and involves the parent waking the child up on the hour during the night. When the child is woken, it is expected that if the child is wet, he or she goes to the toilet and changes the bedding.

There are two types of waking programs. In the regular waking program the parent wakes the child at consecutive time periods, for instance every hour. In the variable waking program, the child is woken at a wide variety of times during the night. There is no regular pattern.

Waking programs are very demanding on the parent and there is no guarantee that the child's brain will link the wakening with his or her own body urges to urinate during the night. A similar comment could be made for the next treatment method to be discussed: dry bed training.

DRY BED TRAINING

There has been some controversy over the ethical application of dry bed training. This procedure involves the child practising correct toileting procedures a large number of times before going to bed, and then lying in bed reciting a statement such as:

'I feel nice and dry in bed.'

In addition to the massed practises (usually 20 times) before going to bed, the child is woken on the hour during the night. Should the child be wet, he or she is to take full responsibility for changing and then to practise again possibly twenty times before returning to sleep.

A study reported by Fincham (1984) reported that parents who had actually implemented a urine alarm program and dry bed training **evaluated the urine alarm procedure as being much more favourable** than the dry bed training. In my experience, dry bed training can be an extremely negative and distressing procedure. Parents can be very grumpy about hourly waking and children can be hysterically upset!

ROLE OF A CONTINENCE PHYSIOTHERAPIST

Some physiotherapists have a special interest in the treatment of bowel and bladder problems in children and adults.

Such a professional working with a child who wets will assess the child's day and night bladder function to determine any physiological basis for the lack of bladder control.

Treatment aims to normalise bladder function. This is done by teaching the child techniques to 'retrain' the bladder both to store urine optimally and empty to completion.

In working towards dryness, a therapist also promotes the child's self-esteem and confidence.

Appropriate physiotherapists may be found by contacting the Continence Foundation of Australia, or the Australian Physiotherapy Association.

CHIROPRACTIC

Chiropractic manipulation has been shown to be effective in some cases of bedwetting. The chiropractor does a careful history and examination before deciding that manipulation is appropriate. The usual form of manipulation is very light and usually applied to the low back area.

Children who have chiropractic manipulation do not experience any discomfort or pain.

HYPNOSIS

Since children under the age of twelve are usually very good hypnotic subjects, it would seem useful to consider the possibility of hypnosis for assisting a child in learning dryness. In my experience, hypnosis is especially useful with older children – children above the age of eight, who are secondary enuretics or who have found their wetting problem to become an increasing source of embarrassment and cause for concern.

Parents are cautioned to seek a therapist who is a qualified and registered hypnotist. I am a member of the Australian Society of Hypnosis. Membership is restricted to medical practitioners, psychiatrists, psychologists and dentists.

I will often make a personalised audiotape, with direct suggestions for the child to integrate mind and body well-being and comfort. Suggestions are also made for increased confidence and positive feelings of self-esteem. In some cases a story might be told on the tape about another child who managed to learn to stay dry or overcame an obstacle that was interfering with their achieving a specific goal. The hypnosis tape may not necessarily be aimed at specific reduction in wetting. A main goal is to assist the child in having calming and confident thoughts prior to sleep and in focussing on achieving any worthwhile aim that they set. Details for arranging for personalised tapes are at the back of this book.

PSYCHOTHERAPY

Long-term psychotherapeutic counselling is not commonly used for treatment of wetting problems. In my experience, children are usually responsive over just a few sessions which concentrate on building self-esteem and boost a sense of personal power over **all** their problems. For ideas to help your child with problem solving and self-esteem, I strongly recommend you read my book *Fear-Free Kids* and listen to my CD *How to Super-Boost Your Child's Self-Esteem*.

BOOKS AND CDs

Some children have become dry simply by reading the children's section of this book! They also enjoy and learn from the *How You Can Be Boss of the Bladder* CD set. The child CD has a story for younger children on one track and on another a positive suggestion track for being dry which is suitable for older children and adults. The CD for parents has information on wetting and becoming dry, and a **BONUS** relaxation track to acknowledge their positive parenting skills and offer a chance to wind down and relax after the busy day (and difficult time fixing up wet beds!).

PROBLEMS AND RELAPSE

Once a child has been reliably dry for two consecutive weeks, continued dryness can be expected. A few children who have cured themselves of wetting with enuresis alarms start wetting again some months later. Usually another training week or two on the alarm will be sufficient to reinstate dryness.

Very, very occasionally, another recurrence of wetting will happen. It may be that there are some changes in the child's life which are not being adjusted to. At this stage it is recommended that the child see a professional for counselling.

Some children relapse during times of stress such as a death in the family, severe sickness, new experiences and changes, such as transition from primary to secondary school or a new baby at home. For some children who relapse, it seems as if their brains just forget the recently learned skill of staying dry. Perhaps the brain and body are too busy integrating new things which have been learned. These children respond best to the alarm program and can usually become dry quickly.

FINAL RECOMMENDATIONS

In the light of the necessity for all treatment methods to be positive and not stressful for the children, parents are initially counselled to use minimally intrusive and maximally positive treatment procedures in order to help their children learn dryness.

Children under the age of five may respond to rewards and a motivation sticker program. **Caution:** Remember, those with primary enuresis (that is, have never had a dry night) may find the reward system frustrating. How can you boss your bladder if your brain and bladder 'won't talk'? Their neurological system is just not ready.

Children over the age of five are ready for a supervised program which typically combines a bell and pad alarm, a motivational scheme, regular weekly telephone calls, and extra drinks after seven consecutive dry nights until fourteen consecutive dry nights are reached. This is the program recommended by the Boss of the Bladder Program. If results for an alarm program with back-up reward scheme are slow to be achieved, progressive awakening and a relaxation CD are often useful additions.

Regular counselling may be appropriate for children on the above programs if there are additional problems such as difficulties with learning, social skills or self-esteem.

APPENDICES

REFERENCES

AZRIN, N.H. & FOXX, R.M. (1974) *Toilet Training in Less Than a Day*, New York, Simon & Schuster.

AZRIN, N.H., SNEED, T.J. & FOXX, R.M. (1974) 'Dry Bed Training: Rapid Elimination of Childhood Enuresis', *Behaviour Research and Therapy*, 12, 147–156.

BALLER, W.R. (1975) *Bedwetting: Origins and Treatment*, New York, Pergamon Press.

BOLLARD, J. & NETTLEBECK, T. (1989) *Bedwetting: A Treatment Manual for Professional Staff*, London, Chapman & Hall.

FINCHAM, F.D. (1984) 'The Social Validation of Behavioural Treatments for Bedwetting', Paper presented at the Fifty-sixth Annual Meeting of the Midwestern Psychological Association, Chicago, Illinois.

HALL, Dr J., for details of all Dr Janet Hall titles see pages 90–94.

HEINS, T. & RITCHIE, K. (1988) *Beating Sneaky Poo, Ideas for Faecal Soiling*, Child & Adolescent Unit, Phillip Health Centre, Corinna St, Phillip, A.C.T. 2606.

KNAPP, Dr M. (1994) Article: 'The Negative Effects of Not Treating Bedwetting', *Australian Doctor Newspaper*.

MACK, A. (1989) *Dry All Night*, Boston, Little, Brown & Co.

MARSHALL, M. (1983) *Mike*, London, The Bodley Head.

MATTHEWS, J. (1994) *Bedwetting: A Manual for Parents*, Melbourne, Ramsey-Coote Instruments.

MEADOW, R. (1980) *Help for Bedwetting*, Churchill, Livingstone.

ROSEN, R. (1980) *I Wet the Bed*, West Melbourne, Thomas Nelson.

SCHAFER, C.E. (1979) *Childhood, Enuresis and Encopresis: Causes and Therapy*, New York, Nostrand Reinhold Co.

WELFORD, H. (1987) *Toilet Training and Bedwetting: A Practical Guide for Today's Parents*, Wellingborough, Thorsons Publishing Group.

USEFUL
INFORMATION

The following article is by Dr Martin Knapp, a consultant physician at North West Regional Hospital (Burnie division) and North West Private Hospital, Burnie, Tasmania. Reprinted with permission from *Australian Doctor Newspaper*.

Enuresis should be regarded as requiring active management because:

1. Toilet accidents have been cited as the secondmost frequent reasons for child abuse.

2. Children are not comfortable with being enuretic, especially with daytime enuresis, which is often associated with odours and name-calling.

Nocturnal enuresis initially causes fewer problems if parental attitudes to wetting are relaxed and accepting.

The potential for nocturnal enuresis to impinge on a child's development increases with age. Avoidance tactics then have to be developed in relation to certain activities, e.g. sleepovers or camping.

It is remarkable with the lifestyle of the older teenager in recent decades that young adults are still presenting for advice.

3. Parents prefer children to reach milestones at the usual times. They often feel anxious or inadequate when bladder control is delayed.

4. There can be conflict between parents and/or carers and the child, especially if they think the condition is in the child's control.

5. There is extra work and cost associated with the extra washing of sheets, nightwear, etc. (daily), extra cleaning (to get rid of bedroom smells) and the replacement of mattresses, nightwear, sheets etc.

It is surprising that parents can be as accepting as they often are when management is so often effective. I consider that enuresis should usually be managed actively. When is active management of enuresis not required? Not very often.

The enuretic child or adolescent, and any parents or carers, need to be persuaded towards active management if they are not of this view.

If there is no motivation to become dry, the management should be directed, after a history and examination, at obtaining motivation.

The selection of the management method may be influenced by a need to overcome some of the reasons for non-motivation.

Resistance to active management often occurs because previous strategies have been wrong or a correct strategy has been inadequately supported.

USEFUL
CONTACTS

States' children's hospitals
Some children's hospitals have clinics for bedwetting, e.g. Royal Children's Hospital, Melbourne, Victoria.

Community hospitals
Outpatients' clinics

Regional community health services

Private agencies
Medical practitioners/paediatricians
Psychologists

Clinics attached to universities
Usually psychology clinics

Continence Foundation of Australia
Resource centres are located in most capital cities and listed in the White Pages directory.

ALARMS

There is a range of alarms available. You should be sure of their compliance with Australian Safety Standards and request information regarding testimonials and recommendations. Also ask for research evidence that supports the effectiveness of the unit.

Some sources are:

1. Advantage Health Care P/L (Dri Control personal alarms)
   34 Percy Street
   Mordialloc
   Victoria 3195
   Australia

2. Farish Bissell Industries P/L (Bell and pad alarms)
   Ms Jill Condie
   P.O. Box 304
   Mt Martha
   Victoria 3934
   Australia

3. Dr Martin Knapp (Malem personal alarms)
   Enuresis Advisory Service
   P.O. Box 354
   Penguin
   Tasmania 7316
   Australia

4. Ramsey-Coote Instruments (Bell and pad alarms)
   18 Edward Street
   Sandringham
   Victoria 3191
   Australia

BOSS OF THE BLADDER
QUESTIONNAIRE ▬▬▬▬▬▬▬▬

This is the questionnaire used in our Boss of the Bladder Program to help assess the current situation. It may be useful to complete for your child to help you choose your next step for treatment.

Parent's Name:

Child's Name: **Child's Age:**

1. Has the child had a complete medical check-up to verify that there is no physical reason for bedwetting? When?

2. Has the child always wet the bed? If not, when did it start?

3. Does wetting only occur at night?

4. How often would you estimate the child wets the bed?

5. How is the problem of the wet bed currently being managed?

6. What had previously been tried to stop bedwetting and how successful was it?

7. How does the child react to a wet bed? How do you feel?

8. Why do you think the child wets the bed?

9. What are the times, moods or conditions when the child is almost certain to:
    (i) Wet the bed?
    (ii) Not wet the bed?

10. How would you rate current motivation to stop the bedwetting?
    (i) Parent motivation   High 1 2 3 4 5 Low
    (ii) Child motivation   High 1 2 3 4 5 Low

11. How do you rate the chances of permanently stopping the bedwetting this time?
    High 1   2   3   4   5   Low

The **BOSS OF THE BLADDER** *Program for Bedwetting*

Stop Wetting ... Save Self-Esteem
(and sheets ... and your washing machine!)

It's winter ... it's raining ... the clothes dryer is already working overtime ... and your little treasure has managed to wet the doona, the sheet, the pillowcase and the PJs (not to mention Teddy) FOR THE FIFTH TIME THIS WEEK!!!
Sound familiar?

FACTS:
- Toilet accidents are the second most frequent reason for child abuse.
- One in ten children up to the age of ten are still wetting the bed.
- Many parents are depressed and are frustrated as to where to go next.
- Parents NEED TO KNOW the facts.
- Children need to understand that their brain can control their bladder and be encouraged to know that wetting is simply a behavioural problem.
- Of the children who attend this clinic, 90% become dry.
- The KEY is a positive, caring treatment program where the child is encouraged to know that dryness is achieved by his or her efforts (not by the parents controlling the child).

HOW THE PROGRAM WORKS:
1. The parents and child are encouraged to read the book: *How to Stop Bedwetting*.

2. A single one-hour interview is arranged to set up the individual program for that child. (Phone consultations can be conducted for long-distance clients.)

3. Parents of young children (older children make their own phone calls) phone the consultant directly each week to give a report.

4. The consultant will outline (by phone) additional strategies as appropriate.

5. Further interviews are made ONLY if necessary and practical.

6. The relaxation CD *How You Can Be Boss of the Bladder* may be recommended. This has been found to be especially useful for older children. It has often been successful – not only for treating bedwetting, but also for helping children improve their concentration and reduce their levels of stress.

COSTS INCLUDE:

One-hour interview, weekly alarm rental and phone monitoring by consultant. Some of the cost may be recoverable from your private health fund. Please check if you are covered for psychology under your private health fund.

The **Boss of the Bladder** *Program*
is a product of Richmond Hill Psychology
111 Hoddle St, Richmond, Victoria 3121, Australia
info@drjanethall.com.au
www.bedwetting.com.au

Comprehensive services offered:
- The BOSS OF THE BLADDER Program
- Books and CDs
- Educational Assessment
- Personality Profiles
- Psychological Counselling
- Success Coaching
- Success Coach Presentations

AUTHOR'S NOTE

We would love to have your comments and suggestions on the usefulness of this book. We would like to hear about your experiences with wetting and dryness.

Relaxation CDs are available on request. These cover general body/brain co-ordination and relaxation to encourage the listener to relax and to stay dry. Personalised CDs can be far more effective and can be arranged at special request.

*ATTENTION: HEALTH PROFESSIONALS
AND PARENT GROUPS*
Dr Janet Hall is available to consult and present in-house talks, seminars and workshops at your venue.

111 Hoddle St, Richmond, Victoria 3121, Australia
info@drjanethall.com.au
www.bedwetting.com.au

DR JANET HALL'S
BOOKS AND CDs

Dr Janet Hall has a uniquely user-friendly way of delivering information. She talks directly to you in everyday, easy to understand terms so that you get maximum benefit in applying her suggested ideas and strategies directly into your life to achieve the success that you deserve.

FAMILY BOOKS

Fear-Free Children

A book which provides a unique insight into the causes, symptoms and treatment of problem fears in children, *Fear-Free Children* shows how fears can be overcome with confidence-building activities, games, stories, self-talk and rewards. *Fear-Free Children* is written in two sections – the first giving information for parents and the second teaching examples through stories for younger children. Teenagers can benefit from reading the entire book and directly applying the information to their own circumstance.

The simplicity makes it easy to understand, adapt and apply so that you quickly get control over your fears and learn to solve your own problems.

Fight-Free Families

Did you know that 85% of families have had their first fight before 9 a.m. in the morning? And they often fight at dinner and especially before bed! *Fight-Free Families* explains why people fight and gives terrific ideas for how to manage fights, but even better – avoid them. It is possible to have an (almost) fight-free family by creating an environment at home that supports the peaceful resolution of conflict.

How You Can Be Boss of Bedtime

Here is an effective solution for all parents who feel frustrated and fed-up when children's bedtime arrives. This book promotes a win-win situation which empowers children to actively plan and participate in their own bedtime routine. The first section of the book is designed for children to read or for it to be read to them. The second section of the book provides parents with information on sleep behaviours and details success strategies which work wonders.

How to Stop Bedwetting

Dr Janet Hall is the founder of the Boss of the Bladder Program in Melbourne, Australia.This book is designed to help both children and parents gain some insight into the management and eventual control of day- and night-wetting.

Children read the first section and are relieved to find out that it's not them who wets on purpose – it's that pesky 'bladder muscle'. Parents are coached in realistic prevention, management and even cure strategies for bedwetting. Everybody boosts their self-esteem when children get dry!

Easy Toilet Training

You will learn the easy procedure for effective toilet training which doesn't make you pull your hair out. You get up-to-date knowledge on the essential steps of toilet training which include timing, readiness and personality differences.

Easy Toilet Training gives step-by-step procedures for effective toilet training with maximum ease and fun for all! After reading this book you will know how to get results quickly, with the least effort and without hiccups.

SexWise: What Every Young Person and Parent Should Know About Sex

This book enrols teenagers in a commitment to responsible sex – choosing the right person, age, place, time, safety and all for the right reasons.

SexWise is a wonderful book for parents because it does all their hard work and saves embarrassment!

GOOD PARENTING CDs

How to Super-Boost Your Child's Self-Esteem

Parents will learn how stress affects parenting, how to offer self-esteem 'damage control', how to identify a 'toxic' parent, how to help your child cope with failure and the three keys to coaching your child towards a solid self-esteem.

Stop Tantrums Now!

You will learn how to handle and prevent tantrums in toddlers (and even some adults!).

The Good Kid Game empowers parents with safety-net procedures for tantrums which produce least fuss and least upset. The Being Ready Routine is great for helping families beat the morning rush without panic, tears and tantrums!

ADULT HYPNOSIS CDs

Did you know that Dr Jan is a very experienced hypnotherapist? She believes very strongly in the power of the mind to assist in boosting your success and she has recorded many CDs which combine Jan's usual style of chatty, easily understood information, with a segment of hypnosis.

You Can Stop Smoking with Hypnosis

You know it's time! This CD will help you to boost your self-esteem and give you the willpower to quit smoking for once and for all!

You Can Lose Weight with Hypnosis

You deserve to have a slim, fit and healthy body. Gain slimness easily and gain confidence in the power of your mind to achieve the results that you deserve.

Heart Healing: How to Heal a Broken Heart and Get On With a Successful Life

What do you do to cope when someone you loved has died or abandoned you?

Track 1 has an explanation of the healthiest way to let go of your upset.

Track 2 gives a unique hypnotic experience which allows your upset to be released and energises you to recommit to your right for maximum personal and relationship success.

You Can Have Total Confidence Through Relaxation

You can super-boost your self-esteem without even trying!

Track 1 gives you a classical relaxation meditation experience where you follow the healing light through your body so that you feel at peace with your world.

Track 2 is a power-boosting and inspiring coaching experience with Dr Jan.

ADULT MOTIVATION AND INFORMATION CDs

How to Stress-Proof Yourself and Succeed ... Faster

With stress-proof coaching you can learn to achieve your goals faster, with no burn-out.

Stop Sexual Harassment! It's Bad for Business!

Sexual harassment can cost millions of dollars with job turn-over expenses, lost productivity and stress-related illness. This CD explains why sexual tension occurs in business and how to promote healthy sexual politics to create and environment that protects your business and investment.

FOR AVAILABILITY OF ALL DR JANET HALL PRODUCTS CONTACT:
Dr Janet Hall
111 Hoddle St, Richmond, Victoria 3121, Australia
www.bedwetting.com.au

Phone: (03) 9419 3010

or

Email: info@drjanethall.com.au

Attention: Health Professionals
For bulk copies of this book at discount prices contact:
The Five Mile Press Pty Ltd
1 Centre Road, Scoresby
Victoria 3179 Australia
www.fivemile.com.au

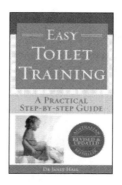

How to Stop
**Bed
Wetting**